Selective Mutism is SO Much more than NOT Speaking.

When parents, treatment professionals and teachers understand Selective Mutism as <u>a social communication anxiety disorder</u>, that's when the 'team approach' begins! With an appropriate treatment plan in place, the child with SM will begin to develop the social confidence and progress across the 'Social Communication Bridge©' into confident verbal communication in all social settings!

By Dr. Elisa Shipon-Blum

Easing School
Jitters
For the Selectively Mute Child

By Dr. Elisa Shipon-Blum

Selective Mutism Anxiety Research and Treatment Center (SMart Center)
505 Old York Rd. Jenkintown, PA 19046
www.selectivemutismcenter.org

ISBN-13: 978-1467921886

Dedication:

I dedicate this book to all parents and educators of children who suffer in silence.

INDEX

Quick Reference

Interactive Work Area

Ask the Doc – FAQ's

Note from Dr. Elisa Shipon-Blum

Social Communication Anxiety Therapy (S-CAT) is the philosophy of treatment developed by international expert, Dr. Elisa Shipon-Blum, and implemented at the Selective Mutism Anxiety Research and Treatment Center (SMart Center) www.selectivemutismcenter.org.

S-CAT is based on the concept that Selective Mutism is a social communication anxiety disorder that is more than just not speaking.

Dr. Shipon-Blum has created the **SM-Stages of Social Communication Comfort Scale** © that describes the various stages of social communication that are possible for a child suffering from Selective Mutism. **The Social Communication Bridge** © illustrates this concept in a visual form.

Children suffering from Selective Mutism (SM) CHANGE their level of social communication based on the setting and expectations from others WITHIN a setting. Therefore social comfort and communication will change from SETTING to SETTING and PERSON TO PERSON.

For example, a child may be 'chatting up a storm' with their friend or perhaps family member in ONE setting, yet see that SAME person in another setting (such as at school or perhaps at a family function) and the child may have difficulty socially engaging, communicating nonverbally and perhaps the child cannot communicate at all!

For some children, they appear VERY comfortable and MUTISM is the most noted symptom. Meaning, they ARE able to engage and have astute nonverbal skills (professional mimes!) in MOST, if not all settings. These children are STUCK in the nonverbal stage of communication (stage 1) and suffer from a subtype of SM called: SPEECH PHOBIA.

Selective Mutism is SO much more than NOT speaking.

'Not speaking' merely touches on the surface of our children! A complete understanding of the child is necessary to develop an appropriate treatment plan (For home and in the Real World) as well as in school by developing accommodations/interventions (i.e. IEP or 504 plan).

According to Dr. Shipon-Blum's work, after a complete evaluation (consisting of various assessment forms-parent/teacher; parent and child interview), treatment needs to address three key questions.

--WHY did a child develop SM? (Influencing, precipitating and maintaining factors)

--WHY does Selective Mutism persist despite being in active treatment and parent/teacher awareness?

And finally,
--WHAT can be done at home, the real world and within school to help the child build the coping skills and overcome their social communication challenges?

To HELP a child suffering in silence an understanding of which stage the child is IN during particular social encounters. The **Social Communication Anxiety Inventory (SCAI)** can be used to determine the stage of social communication.

Treatment is THEN developed via the WHOLE child approach where, under the direction of the outside treatment professional, the child, parents and school personnel work together. Dr. Shipon-Blum emphasizes that although anxiety lowering is key it is often NOT enough, especially as children age. Over time, many children with Selective Mutism no longer feel 'anxious' but mutism and often lack of proper social engagement continues to exist in select settings.

Children with SM need strategies/interventions to progress from nonverbal to spoken communication. This is the TRANSITIONAL stage of communication and interestingly enough, It is this aspect that is often missing from most treatment plans. In other words, HOW do you help a child progress from NONVERBAL to verbal communication?

Quite frankly, time in the therapy office is simply NOT enough. The office setting is used to help prepare the child for the outside world. Strategies and interventions are developed based on WHERE the child is on the SOCIAL COMMUNICATION BRIDGE and are meant to be a desensitizing method as well as a vehicle to UNLEARN conditioned behavior and to develop coping skills to combat social communication anxiety.

S-CAT incorporates anxiety lowering techniques, methods to build self-esteem and strategies/interventions to help with social comfort and communication progression, such as 'Bridging' from shut down to nonverbal communication and then TRANSITIONING into spoken communication via verbal intermediaries, ritual sound shaping and possibly the use of augmentative devices etc.

The KEY concept that children with SM need to understand, feel in control and have choice in their treatment (age dependent) are a critical component of S-CAT.

S-CAT provides CHOICE to the child and helps to transfer the child's NEED for control INTO the strategies and interventions!

Therefore GAMES and GOALS (based on age) via the use of ritualistic and controlled methods (I.e., use of strategy charts) are used to help develop social comfort and progress into speech.

Silent goals (environmental changes; parent education, school staff education, school based accommodations/interventions) and active goals (child directed goals based on CHOICE and CONTROL) are used within the S-CAT program.

Every child is different and therefore an individualized treatment plan needs to be developed that incorporates HOME (parent education, environmental changes), Addressing the child's unique needs and SCHOOL (teacher education, accommodations/interventions).

Therefore, by lowering anxiety, increasing self-esteem as well as increasing communication and social confidence within a variety of REAL WORLD settings, the child suffering in silence will develop necessary coping skills to enable for proper social, emotional and academic functioning.

SELECTIVE MUTISM-STAGES OF SOCIAL COMMUNICATION COMFORT SCALE ©

NON-COMMUNICATIVE -neither non-verbal nor verbal. **NO social engagement.**

STAGE 0 - NO Responding, NO initiating

Child stands motionless (stiff body language), expressionless, averts eye gaze, appears 'frozen,' **MUTE**
OR
Seemingly IGNORES person while interacting or speaking to other(s). **MUTE towards others**

For communication to occur, **Social Engagement** must occur

COMMUNICATIVE (Nonverbal and/or Verbal*)

*TO ADVANCE FROM ONE STAGE OF COMMUNICATION TO THE NEXT, INCREASING SOCIAL COMFORT NEEDS TO OCCUR.

STAGE 1 - Nonverbal Communication: (NV)

1A Responding -pointing, nodding, writing, sign language, gesturing, use of 'objects' (e.g. whistles, bells, Non-voice augmentative device (e.g. communication boards/cards, symbols, photos)

1B Initiating -getting someone's attention via pointing, gesturing, writing, use of 'objects' to get attention (e.g. whistles, bells, Non-voice augmentative device (e.g. communication boards/cards, symbols, photos)

STAGE 2 - Transition into Verbal Communication (TV)

2A Responding -Via any <u>sounds,</u> **(**e.g. grunts, animal sounds, letter sounds, moans, etc.): <u>Verbal Intermediary</u> or Whisper Buddy; <u>Augmentative Device with sound,</u> (e.g. simple message switch, multiple voice message device, tape recorder, video, etc.)

2B Initiating -Getting someone's attention via any <u>sounds,</u> (e.g. grunts, animal sounds, letter sounds, moans., etc.): <u>Verbal Intermediary</u> or Whisper Buddy; <u>Augmentative Device with sound,</u> (e.g. , simple message switch, multiple voice message device ,tape recorder, video, etc)

STAGE 3 - Verbal Communication (VC)

3A Responding – Approximate speech/direct speech (e.g. altered or made-up language, baby talk, reading/rehearsing script, soft whispering, speaking)

3B Initiating - Approximate speech/direct speech (e.g. altered or made-up language, baby talk, reading/rehearsing script, soft whispering, speaking)

BRIDGE TO COMMUNICATION

SMart Center

Selective Mutism Anxiety Research & Treatment Center

NAME: _____

REAL WORLD _____

SCHOOL_____

**SOCIAL COMMUNICATION BRIDGE ©
for SELECTIVE MUTISM**

Verbal (stage 3)

____ Quiet speaking

____ Script approach

____ Altered speech

Transitional (stage 2)

SOCIAL ENGAGEMENT!

Nonverbal (stage 1)

____ VERBAL INTERMEDIARY

(1) 'TELL ME'

(2)	Close Up	Fist length	1/2 arm length	Full arm length

____ SOUNDS (Ritual Sound Approach) (RSA)

SOUNDS————————————>WORDS

SSS
HHH —>S=yes—>Y+S=YES—>SIT —> Ans. Q's
PPP   PIT
WW   CAT

____ AUGMENTATIVE DEVICES

Noncommunicative (stage 0)

____ Nodding

____ Pointing/Gesturing

____ Writing

____ Frontline!

____ Handover/Takeover

____ Waving

Increasing Social Comfort & Communication————>

This book is designed to help parents, teachers and therapists' support and guide children who have Selective Mutism, teaching them to cope with the stressful feelings they experience in school. With these tactics, along with <u>proper therapy</u>, there is every reason to believe that Selectively Mute children can succeed in school, beat their anxiety disorder, and enjoy their school days to the fullest!

For the majority of children, going to school is filled with exciting anticipation and joy…seeing old friends, making new friends, learning tons of new stuff, being out of the house and having fun…but for the Selectively Mute child, back-to-school can be terrifying!

As most of us already know, well over 90% of Selectively Mute children have social phobia in addition to Selective Mutism. These children actually feel like they are on stage almost every minute of the day! Just imagine what this is like…pure fear from morning until afternoon. These children are so fearful that they literally cannot speak!

The anxiety and tension that results from this can be very debilitating for most children, day in and day out. Tension, anxiety, fearfulness, and apprehension are just a few of the many emotions that SM children experience. Many, if not all, eventually have significant physical symptoms that accompany their anxiety; headaches, stomachaches, dizziness, nausea, diarrhea and joint pains are a few examples. In addition, SM children often manifest symptoms of other anxiety disorders, such as fears, phobias, generalized worries, panic and obsessive/compulsive symptoms like hoarding. The array of anxious feelings that the typical SM child feels is well beyond the obvious 'lack of speaking.'

These children are not lying, pretending, manipulating, or attempting to seek attention; they are actually feeling these symptoms. As our children get older, they often feel alone and withdrawn, believing they are the only ones experiencing these feelings.

> **Anxiety can be so severe for the SM child that just the thought of going to school and confronting other children and teachers may be enough to bring on an array of physical symptoms.**

It is quite common for SM children to be misunderstood. Mutism is frequently perceived as oppositional, controlling and willful behavior. Unfortunately, these perceptions are anything but correct. These grave misconceptions only propagate anxiety and often lead to inaccurate assessments and evaluations as well as mismanagement in the school setting. It is important to understand that Selective Mutism is a means of avoiding anxious feelings precipitated by social interaction and expectations from others. Just as a person who is afraid or fearful of heights cannot comfortably go to the top of a tall building and look over, nor can a child with Selective Mutism speak with comfort in various social settings and they may even be unable to communicate nonverbally. Understanding that Selective Mutism is a true anxiety disorder is the first step in helping the anxious child who **'has trouble getting the words out'** begin to overcome their communication fears.

We can now begin *easing school jitters* for our anxious, often silent children; who, by the way, are anything but quiet at home and when comfortable!

HELPING TO RELIEVE STRESS!

The MOST important thing for any child is to feel *SAFE, SECURE,* and

CONFIDENT.

If your child is old enough to express his/her fears, my advice would be to sit down and talk to your child about his/her 'inability to get the words out. Letting your child know you are there for him/her and that you understand it is hard 'to get the words out' at times is a huge relief for children. **Children MUST be helped to understand why they cannot speak.** They must acknowledge their anxiety and mutism. Therefore, talking about their feelings and anxiety and putting a name to their 'inability to speak' gives the SM child feelings of control, which they desperately need! For our young preschoolers and early elementary aged children, knowing they have 'selective mutism' is not as important as knowing that they 'have a hard time getting the words out'. Then it is crucial to work with a professional who can help them figure out their feelings when they are mute. As children get older, knowing the term, 'selective mutism' may be helpful and a solace to know there is a TERM for their inability to verbalize and communicate comfortably. Again, our children need feelings of control, the more they are involved and understand, the greater their ability to overcome their communication anxiety.

Our children MUST be helped to understand WHY they cannot speak and they must begin to acknowledge how they feel in a variety of social situations.

Parents will agree that as soon as their child KNEW there was a name for WHY they could not get the words out, it was as if a ton of bricks were lifted off of their child's shoulders! This cannot be emphasized enough.

It is very confusing and frustrating to a child when all of his/her peers, family and 'the rest of the world' seem to speak so easily, and yet he or she cannot. Over time, without knowing or understanding, denial and avoidance begin. This is demonstrated by the child who avoids talking about it or insists he/she will NOT speak and does not speak. Experience shows that children who deny their mutism have built up a **wall of defense.** Therefore, in order for a child to overcome their anxiety, they must first acknowledge their mutism and express their feelings about the anxiety they experience. Since Selectively Mute children are notorious for '***holding back their feelings***' and keeping things inside, this process is that much more important! Helping a child open up to their fears, thoughts and worries and overall feelings about school is a great way to begin finding out what your child really feels. With this in mind……….Find a time when you and your child can sit and talk about his/her **FEELIINGS** regarding school. Begin by emphasizing the positives: ask your child to tell you about what they LIKE about school and make a list.

Begin to help your child recognize and talk about feelings they get when they are in a 'mute' and anxious setting. Most children do not know WHY they do not speak, nor do they know HOW they feel. Therefore, the goal is to help the child figure this out. From working with countless children, I have come to realize that the majority feel 'scared', although some do not associate the feelings with fear but instead describe it as 'hard' to get the words out. Ask your child if this is how it feels, and it will start the process. Help your child RATE or GRADE their feelings of anxiety in various situations. Grading feelings between 0→5 or using visual images such as a stack of blocks, are useful ways that our children can begin to understand their feelings from one situation to the next. **Parents should work with children frequently to help them 'assess' their feelings.**

My favorite things to do in school:

(1) Play with friends

(2) Go to science class to learn about different animals

(3) Doing artwork

(4) Playing on the playground with Jonny, Adam & Zachary at recess

Encourage your child to TALK about RECESS.
Talk about how fun recess is! Talk about the friends they love to play with, their favorite monkey bars, or swinging on the swings! Do this with every 'favorite' thing they like to do. Then, begin alternating the list with things they do not like about school. Have them elaborate on what it is about that 'not-so-good' thing that makes them uncomfortable. Then, with your

child, come up with ideas as to what would make that 'terrible-thing...not so terrible'. The idea here is to make your child realize that they do like things about school, and that things are not as scary as they might think. They will come to see that there are ways to make the 'not-so good things' better and that school is not such a bad place after all!

Talking to your child helps him/her verbalize their inner most feelings. When your child holds in his/her feelings, anxiety actually increases and builds up as the child's innermost feelings and fears are 'buried'. By opening up and expressing emotions, children are confronting fears, concerns, etc., which in turn, decreases stress!

EASING THE BACK TO SCHOOL JITTERS!!

After speaking to many children, I have compiled a list of the **biggest fears children have regarding school.** Using this information, I have created this list of ways to **"Ease the jitters:"**

 Afraid of their new teacher

This is a common fear, especially among younger children. To help overcome this, I recommend finding out ahead of time who the teacher will be and visiting the school before the year begins.

Spend time in the classroom with the teacher so the room doesn't seem so foreign to your child. Call the teacher in advance and tell him/her that it would make your child more comfortable if they could meet before the start of school. Consider also inviting your child's teacher to come to your home! If this is not possible, plan to go to the classroom and talk with the teacher. Allow your child to just relax and play there. Playing interactive games in the classroom such as computer and board games where your child can participate without having to speak (and where eye contact is minimized) are excellent ways to build rapport without expectations and pressure to 'communicate.'

Perhaps your child can help the teacher set up the classroom! During these visits, make sure there is no pressure to verbalize. *You* can just chat with the teacher about his or her life, which will help your child to realize that the teacher is a real person with a real life. Perhaps the teacher is a parent with kids of his/her own. You would be surprised how realizing that their teacher is 'a person too' can relieve a significant amount of stress!

 Meeting new people

Discuss with your child what, exactly, makes them nervous about this. Talk to them about how you felt as a child when you had to meet new children. Believe it or not, letting your child know that you, too, had similar fears actually takes the 'mystery' out of their worries and makes them feel they are not alone. Talking honestly about your fears and how you handle these feelings is a great tactic to use with your children.

Parents often tend to GIVE ADVICE. For example, in regard to meeting new friends, many parents will innocently tell their child to sit near certain children, to try to talk to the other kids, or to play with them in the playground.

For the typical SM child this advice can cause a great deal of inner stress and turmoil. The child wants to please his/her parent, but at the same time feels that initiating conversation or even play is an impossible feat. MOST SM children cannot easily approach other children, wave to them or smile at them. **In fact, it is rare for the typical SM child to initiate communication at all** when in anxious social settings, unless it is with a very close friend or other 'comfortable' person. A parent's advice will only make the child feel badly if they cannot accomplish what is suggested. Recommendations would be to focus on what your child CAN do. Talk about different situations that may arise in school and list ideas that might make these situations more comfortable. Role-playing, with parent (or a puppet, doll, or stuffed animal) playing the part of the SM child, is an excellent way to come up with these ideas! Talking about your child's present friends and discussing and acting out ways to 'get to know' other children will help your child much more than TELLING your child what to do. In addition, speak to the teacher and other children's parents to set up situations that will enable social encounters to occur more easily. Figure out ways to set your child up to succeed with small goals toward socializing!

 Scared about not being liked by the other kids

This is a very common fear for children with SM. Recommendations would be to talk to them about the friends they DO have, emphasizing how much these friends like your child and why. List some of the fun things he/she does with friends, and point out that there is a good chance many of the other children in their class have similar interests and like the same things! SM children, contrary to some people's beliefs are very social beings. They crave friendships and relationships  with other children, but due to their anxiety, are often unable to respond to other children's offers to play and often cannot initiate play. This can be quite frustrating to the SM child who desperately wants friends, but just has a hard time breaking the ice.

There are specific ways that parents can help the process of building relationships. Very often a parent will state their child has at least one or two very good friends. Upon examination of the history of the relationship between the SM child and their 'best friends,' it becomes obvious that these relationships started a while back where the children were engaged in play, often and usually at the SM child's home. In many cases these friendships began out of convenience (A neighbor friend who was an easy play date at a young age? Perhaps a child of a parent's friend?) Relationships grew over time, but not without time and effort. Therefore, the best way to help the SM child build friendships is to begin with one child at a time at the SM child's home. Make a list of children that your child would like to get to know better. Tell your child that he/she can invite some of these new kids over to play, and that you will be happy to call their moms to set up play dates. This will elate MOST children! What you are doing is helping your child build friendships in a manner that feels safe and secure for him/her (on his 'home turf"); hence setting your child up for success!

 Not knowing their way around the school

 Help relieve this fear by touring the school, walking around to find the classroom, lunchroom, library, gym, etc. Do this quite a few times until your child can get to each place on his/her own! If you are going to drive your child to school, I suggest actually getting up early a few mornings and 'pretending' it is time for school. This *game* works well with younger children. Then drive to school and literally walk to the classroom and throughout the building and grounds. In the majority of cases, children will feel relieved that you are going to take them to 'get-to-know' the school prior to the start of school.

It is important to TALK to your child throughout the building. Since few people are around in the summer or after school, your child may be able to start talking to you within the school in a rather short time.

 Not being smart enough

This is a common fear among ALL children but even more so for the typical SM child who may be a perfectionist. It is common for children with SM to fear bringing attention to himself/herself, and to worry about making mistakes. One way to help counter these fears is to emphasize your child's positive attributes! If your child is a strong reader, or great writer, tell him/her this. Interestingly enough, experience with countless SM children has taught me that most are quite bright, inquisitive, perceptive and sensitive. Talk to them about how well they read and/or write and mention how proud you are of them. Help your child to build his/her skills even more! Go to the bookstore or library and allow him/her to choose books, buy math and reading workbooks and encourage practicing academic skills. Have your child read to you, to younger siblings, etc. Encourage writing, reading and math as much as possible, until he/she feels confident and secure with these skills!

Emphasize your child's positives in order to build their CONFIDENCE

Worrying what others will say or do when they are 'unable to speak'

This is a very common concern among SM children, especially as they get older. Something as easy as speaking is virtually impossible for our SM children. Therefore insecurity and frustration and eventually denial and avoidance may occur. This is an excellent situation for 'talk therapy.' It is important to explain to your child that everyone has something that is difficult for him or her to do. Indicate that although others may be able to 'get the words out' easier at times, there are many things that your child excels at. For example, when talking with your child say, *"YES, it is hard for you to 'get the words out' at times, but think of all of the great things you can do!"* Making a list of talents and things that your child can do well is a wonderful way for him/her to see his/her positive attributes.

SM children often have concerns over how to address others when comments are made about their mutism; it is important to discuss ways in which the SM child can communicate to other children how they feel about their mutism. Since initiating conversation may be difficult, even among the closest of friends in school, encourage letter writing among children; this is an excellent way for our children to let their friends know exactly how they feel.

```
Dear Eva,
Remember when you asked me why I do not talk to the teacher, well,
it is because it is hard for me to talk sometimes. Just like it is
hard for you to spell words. Talking is hard for me, but spelling
is easy for me. So, that is why I have a hard time talking
sometimes. But, I do talk a lot when I am at home, just not at
school.
                                                    Love, Katie
```

Others hearing their voice;
"Will the other kids laugh?" "Will the teacher make a big deal over hearing my voice?"

Many SM children have a great deal of concern about the reaction that others might have to hearing their voice. Again, 'talk therapy' should be used to help your child overcome negative assumptions. "And WHAT IF they laugh? What if they make a big deal? What can possibly happen?" This process of thinking through 'worries' and coming up with ways to combat those worries is a form of cognitive behavioral therapy (CBT). A treating professional trained in CBT is a wonderful aid in helping your child see things in a more positive manner. Making a list of worse case scenarios and best case scenarios about other individual's reactions when their voice is heard is wonderfully therapeutic and provides excellent discussion material. Goals are for your child to SEE that in reality it is not SO BAD that others hear their voice. This concept will need much reiteration on your part as well as when working with a professional. It is also generally helpful to talk to your child's teacher and perhaps his/her classmates about not making a big deal if they hear the SM child's voice.

Quick Reference
TACTICS
To build confidence and self-esteem, and to help your child view school as a positive, non-frightening place to be

Go to the school and meet the teacher, principal and other 'authority-figures' before the school year starts.

Go there as many times as you can. Go to the classroom when the teacher is not there too. Stay in the classroom and allow your child to SPEAK to you in the room, engaging them in conversation. I recommend bringing a friend (or two!) so you can engage your child in conversation with other (comfortable) children as well.
Having your child VERBALIZE in their actual classroom allows them to see themselves as talkers there. **It is very important for children to realize that they CAN talk in the classroom!**

Picking the particular teacher for the SM child should be a joint decision between parent and school.

This decision is a crucial one! The teacher can make or break the entire year in terms of the SM child's ability to progress communicatively. The teacher must be educated to the truths about SM and the parent should feel secure that the teacher is willing to enable much parent involvement. The SM child needs a nurturing and calm teacher who is willing to 'take that extra step' in flexibility and support. Teachers and school personnel need to understand the importance of your child getting to know the teacher prior to the start of school.   Fortunately, most teachers are more than willing to meet the child. Many will come to the home or meet with you in a park if you request that. Meeting the teacher, and having your child spend one on one time alone with the teacher will help your child feel more comfortable than meeting the teacher with a group of children around. Having your child meet the teacher a month or so prior to school is an excellent way to 'EASE THE JITTERS.'   Perhaps the teacher will allow your child to help set up the classroom for the start of school! This is a great stress reliever, and your child will feel proud of her/his efforts.

 Get your child involved in some sort of physical activity.

Studies clearly indicate that regular physical activity stimulates the 'feel-good' chemicals in the brain. Studies confirm that physically active children do better in school and are more alert than non-physically active children. Try to pick a sport or activity that you believe your child will succeed in.   Building up a particular skill is a great self-esteem booster! Encouraging an activity where your child can participate in non-competitive setting and being grouped with a close friend (or two!) will help your child feel more comfortable.

 Since children often play sports in school during recess or gym class, children will often feel self-assured and proud of themselves when they are able to perform and do well in a particular sport!! For boys this is often more crucial than for girls, since performing at recess by playing a sport is very common for our young men. Therefore, helping boys, young and old, feel confident on the playing field with their peers is very important. Some back yard games with Dad, an older brother/sister, relative or neighbor are a great way to build up skills and increase confidence for time with the 'guys' during school! In fact, taking the child TO THE SCHOOL on weekends/holidays and/or after school is a great way to build comfort right there on the school grounds.

 Pursue an activity in which your child can excel.

For example, if your child enjoys gymnastics, try to enroll him/her in classes. Help your child excel in a particular sport or activity that clearly sets them apart from the other children. This will help them feel proud and confident when they master certain skills. **Many SM children like art.** Is this a coincidence? I do not think so! Because SM children do not verbalize as much as other children, they often learn to express themselves creatively through drawing, writing and creating! Go with this

and encourage their interests! Let your child know how proud you are of him/her! Frame your child's art and display the artwork in your home. The excitement this brings is tremendous! In addition (if your child is comfortable with this), the 'masterpieces' can be a topic of conversation when guests are over! If your child loves music, perhaps he/she would want to 'perform a show' for you or the entire family. Interestingly enough, when working with older SM children, it is often the 'special interest' that has been the area where the child has blossomed the most socially and communicatively! Why? Because this was the area where confidence was the highest!

Encouraging a talent and boosting self-esteem create a WIN-WIN situation in every respect!

 Encourage as much socialization as possible!

Small, frequent gatherings are the best approach. Invite friends over, have holiday parties, have Sunday barbecues: In other words, engage your child in as many social functions as possible. No matter how or when you plan these social events, what is important is to **just do it!** Get your child accustomed to being around as many people as possible, but **DO NOT PRESSURE TO SPEAK.** Just allow them to be there. Having gatherings at the child's home is an ideal way to socialize; however, going out of the house is recommended as well. Suggestions would be to prepare your child well in advance, encourage your child to bring along a friend. Arrive places early and if possible check out locations prior to parties or gatherings. With correct planning, parents will be amazed at how their child will slowly become increasingly comfortable in social settings!

 Volunteer in the classroom from the start of school

Allow your child to see you at school. Your presence is a comfort for them. Volunteer and be as involved as you can! Many children will whisper to parents and even talk when a parent is in the classroom. Our goal is for your child to have a lowered anxiety level so communication and eventually verbalization and relaxation will soon occur in the classroom. Each time that you visit, your child will become increasingly more comfortable. A suggestion would be as your child is whispering to you, gradually move further and further away from him/her, so that they need to whisper LOUDER.

 Encourage good EATING and SLEEPING habits! Early to bed, early to rise!

A well-rested child is more relaxed, comfortable, and accommodating than a tired one! Good eating habits, and regular nutritious meals and snacks allow for a constant energy level. Too many sweets cause fatigue (later in the day) and irritability in some children. Studies clearly indicate that an 'exhausted' child is more irritable, more anxious, has lowered attention span, and is more easily distracted and impulsive. Having Selective Mutism is enough to contend with, but adding more issues will only perpetuate anxiety.

 Talk to your

This cannot be emphasized enough! Validate their feelings and concerns. Help them come up with ways to 'make things better' by **emphasizing positives**! This will help lessen stress, and at the same time, allow them to feel closer to you. For children who are willing to discuss their mutism, this is very positive. Once feelings are out in the open, children often feel quite relieved and less anxious.

 If your child looks worried, ask a lot of questions.

Selectively Mute children are notorious for holding in their feelings. They often have difficulty expressing their inner thoughts and worries, which, in turn, may exacerbate their anxiety level. Parents of young children often say that their child has minimal worries; however, younger children may not yet be able to express their inner thoughts and concerns. They often manifest stress through negative behavior at home. Irritability, frequent crying, defiance, not listening, stubbornness, and other difficult behaviors are often signs of inner stress. As children get older more generalized anxiety symptoms emerge. At this point, the child might talk about fears and exhibit frequent worrying.

Some common worries are: death, fires, bombs, terrorist attacks, parents leaving and not coming back, being left alone, getting lost, nighttime, darkness, monsters, etc.

KEEP AN OPEN PATH OF COMMUNICATION

Helping your child to
get to know other children
in a non-threatening manner

 Contact the school to determine which children will be in your child's new class.

Call the parents and **schedule play dates** with different children. Start out with one child, then once your child is communicating and hopefully verbalizing comfortably with that child, invite another, then another, and so on. Eventually have two, three, four or more children over at the same time. Again, the idea is to build a comfort level with a variety of children, and verbalization may carry over to the school. SM children typically have a difficult time 'initiating' play and 'breaking the ice' with other children so parents will often need to help younger children interact.

When the new friend comes to your home, you may want to help your child interact with him/her. This can be done quite subtly. Baking, board games, and doing crafts together with the children will help your child feel more comfortable. Also, chances are, since you are nearby, your child will feel more secure and less anxious.

Suggest and plan for such activities as puppet shows, dress up and make-believe games. Surprisingly enough, SM children are often able to communicate well (possibly even verbalizing) by using make-believe voices or 'acting' like someone else.

Encourage your child to write a letter, draw a picture, or e-mail his/her new friend.

Take children, who will be in your child's class, to the school during the summer, during after school hours, or on the weekends.

Start out with one child. When your child is communicating quite readily to this one child, invite another to go along. Increase to a few kids at one time accompanying you to the school and classroom.
Bring workbooks and have the children 'play school' right there in the classroom!

Practice on the **playground!**

Allow your child to play as much as possible outside in the school playground or playing field. The goal is to desensitize your child to the school playground. Bring friends along. These should be the same friends with whom your child is having play dates!

Try to use these tips as examples, and modify them for your child. Obviously these are not 'miracle cures.' However, building self-confidence and easing stress, together with proper therapy, love and encouragement, are wonderful building blocks for your child's overall success in school and in overcoming Selective Mutism!

Interactive Work Area

The following few pages are meant to help you interact with your child in a positive and fun manner. Encouraging your child to draw, color and/or write can bring out feelings, thoughts and worries.

Depending on the age of your child, you can encourage him/her to write or draw in this interactive section. As long as both you and your child are happy and relaxed, and communication is being accomplished, you are on the right track to helping your child relieve inner anxiety and pent up fears, and ultimately overcoming Selective Mutism.

The point of this guide is to enable your child to see school in a fun and exciting way. Negative thoughts should not be discouraged but can be balanced with positive discussion. Encourage conversation about each item, and if anything negative comes up in conversation, try to bring out the positive in the situation and help your child to see things in a more productive manner.

I like school because:

Friends I like to play with are:

Taking the bus to school is fun because:

Things that I like to do in school:
(1)

(2)

(3)

Things that I am really good at:
(1)

(2)

(3)

I like my teacher because:

I know my teacher likes me because:

When my friends and I are in school, we like to:

Going to school is important because:

I know my friends like me because:

My favorite things to do after school are:

When friends come over to my house we like to:

When I grow up I want to be:

I am special because:

My favorite things I like about me are:

(1)

(2)

(3)

I am good at so many things. The things I am the best at are:
(1)

(2)

(3)

ASK THE DOC
Frequently Asked Questions

(1) My son seems to like school, but when we go in the morning, he tends to cling to me and has a blank, expressionless face. He looks like a statue! Why does this happen?

What you are describing is the typical 'SM look.' Reasons for this are due to 'anxiety' and the effects anxiety has on our children's bodies. When anxious, our children get the 'fear' look, similar to a frightened animal in the wild. Certain areas of the brain are stimulated when in anxious situations, and this causes a variety of responses; one of which is muscle stiffening. Since the face is lined with muscle, our children's blank look is a direct reflection of skeletal muscle tension. This has nothing to do with their liking of school or any other situation, just a manifestation of anxiety

(2) The frozen appearance (as described in (1) above) was present at the beginning of the school year and right after holiday breaks and long weekends. Seems that as the spring is approaching, I am seeing less and less of that 'look.' Does this mean anxiety is less?

Yes. Our children tend to be most anxious during transition times (start of new school year or returning back to school after being home for a holiday or illness). Interestingly enough, as the school year progresses and our children become more comfortable with their teachers, classmates and school environment, that 'fearful' frozen-look dissipates. You will also notice that as the 'look' dissipates our children tend to communicate better. This might be in the form of nonverbal communication comfort, but nevertheless, communication often begins to occur. It should be noted that as the school year progresses and the look goes away, unless the child is involved in treatment to help build communication skills, that 'look' may reappear at the beginning of the next school year, and the same scenario will reoccur.

(3) We have four SM children in our school district. The younger elementary students seem to 'shut down' and get that blank, frozen look, yet the older SM students are mute but appear more relaxed in school. Is this common?

From working with Selectively Mute children of all ages, I have noticed that the 'frozen-look' is much more common in younger children. Although older children and teens can portray that anxious look, it certainly is not nearly as common. Reasons for this are that as time goes on, our children learn to adjust and feel more comfortable in social environments, such as school. From years of being in a social environment, they develop methods of coping. However if they are still mute, they have not developed the coping skills to be able to communicate effectively.

(4) My daughter can speak easily to her best friend everywhere but school. The second my daughter is in school, she cannot even whisper to her friend. My daughter tells me that she just 'can't get the words out' in school. Is this common and what can I do to help?

This scenario is very common. In fact, for the majority of young SM children this happens quite often. Your child's anxiety is heightened within the school environment. Her anxiety is stifling and crippling her to the point that she is mute with her friend and unable to speak. To build verbal comfort with her friend in school, I suggest beginning with a play date at home, where verbalization is occurring freely, and then transferring the play date to the school (start off on the playground or grounds, then into the classroom). Ideally this should eventually occur with few others around. Chances are that since your child has been speaking to her friend easily, speaking will continue since there are minimal outside pressures. I suggest doing this often and consistently so that your child can 'see' herself as a speaker with her friend within school. As this scenario becomes easier and easier for your child, your treating professional should help your child progress to whispering and communicating during the school session.

(5) My son's friend is upset with him because my son <u>won't</u> talk to him in school. He and other children are always trying to get my son to talk in school. How can I help?

First off, your son **CAN'T** talk in school; it is not that he WON'T talk in school. Anxiety is high and your son becomes communicatively impaired. I suggest talking to your son first. Let him know that you understand. Let him know that although speaking is hard and can be scary at times, everyone has something that is difficult. I suggest making a list with your son of things he can do well and easily. Talk about this openly and let your son express his feelings to you. Then, once he is comfortable, he can either approach his friend/s (if he is old enough and feels comfortable) or you can talk with the other child and your son together. Explain to your son's friend that 'talking' in school is hard right now, and that your son's inability to talk has nothing to do with his friendship and liking towards him or other friends. Ask your son's friend

31

to think about something that is hard for him, and then compare that to your son's inability to get the words out easily in school. With regard to other children in the class; talk with your child's teacher about this same concept. There is a FAQ in the book "The Ideal Classroom Setting for the Selectively Mute Child" that deals specifically with ways to handle the curious ones in the class that do not understand an SM child's silence. Having other children identify with feelings of their own that can compare to how an SM child may feel is an excellent way to get the point across and explain why children with SM are unable to speak at times.

(6) My child says she does not speak at school because she doesn't like the sound of her voice. Yet, she talks, sings and yells quite confidently at home. In fact, she often sings at the top of her voice in the grocery store (until someone approaches her then she shuts down). Is it common for SM children to say that they do not like their voice?

Interestingly enough, there are some SM children who say this very same thing... that they do not like the sound of their voice. Reasons for this vary from truly not liking their voice, having been told they 'talk funny' or are 'hard to understand' to just coming up with a reason as to why they are mute. A suggestion would be to try speech therapy. Working with a speech and language pathologist can help build verbal confidence and may help your child tremendously! Along with the speech therapy, working with a treating professional who can help with other anxiety lowering techniques, such as practicing verbalization in the school with you before and after school, having frequent play dates with children from the class, bringing those kids into class before and after school, etc....are all examples of how to help your SM child feel more socially confident and comfortable.

(7) My son has been invited to a birthday party for one of his school friends at a nearby bowling alley. He indicates that he wants to go, but experience tells me that the day will come and my son will not want to go. And, if we do go, he will stand in the corner alone unable to interact with others. Then, as the party is over, he will start interacting with his friends. I am not sure how to handle this situation.

This is such a common occurrence for our SM children. First off, your child WANTS to go to the party. Since the majority of SM children have social anxiety symptoms, the day of the party often elicits anxious feelings at the thought of interacting in a social setting. Since our children need a very long 'warm-up' period it often takes the entire duration of some parties for some of our children to feel less anxious and ready to interact. This is typical.

Suggestions would be to:

- Far in advance, talk to your child about the events and location of the party. If not too far, perhaps visit the party location. Perhaps plan on bowling one afternoon or weekend prior to the party!
- The day of the party, arrive very early before the majority of the children arrive. Walking into a crowded room is difficult. Minimizing this as much as possible will only help your child. Plus, since 'warm-up' time takes a while, the earlier it starts, the better!
- Bring along a friend! Nothing like going somewhere with a buddy. ☺
- If, on the day of the party, you do all of the above and your son is still clingy and mute, suggestions would be to just support your child, stay close by and praise them for their brave efforts of going to the party.

(8) My 7 yr old daughter has told us that she does not want to speak and is not going to speak until she is in college. Isn't this oppositional behavior?
At first sight, this most certainly seems like the words of an oppositional child. However, having worked with so many SM children, I have come to realize that SM children are not oppositional with their mutism. What happens is that when a child is mute and unable to speak, he/she develops maladaptive methods of coping. Avoidance and denial tend to prevail if the child does not understand why, unlike everyone else; she cannot get the words out. It is easier to state what this child has stated, than to confront something that is completely perplexing to her….mutism. This child does not understand WHY she does not speak, nor does she have any clue HOW to figure out her feelings. She is in complete denial. She needs to work with a treating professional who can help her begin to acknowledge and assess her feelings. Once this occurs, then she is ready to begin treatment.

(9) My child has recently been diagnosed with Selective Mutism. What type of professional can help her?
What is important is finding someone who UNDERSTANDS; whether this is a psychologist, social worker, speech pathologist, physician, etc. In other words, as long the treating professional understands the dynamics of Selective Mutism and is able to develop a treatment plan based on her unique situation, then you should be in excellent hands! The team approach is also a must. In other words, coordinating home and school is KEY e.g., working on ways to build communication and social comfort begins with forming friendships with other children. While you are having play dates with specific children, the school is arranging

specific social situations involving that child and your child. Your treating professional will be guiding the process along.

(10) My child recently was evaluated for school placement. I was told she scored in the below average IQ range. I am shocked since my child seems so bright and inquisitive at home! How can this be possible?

Actually it is quite common for our anxious children to test poorly. Especially if there was verbal and timed testing. Since our children are unable to speak in many testing situations, inexperienced evaluators may mark answers wrong if there is no verbal response. Secondly, when anxious, our children may hesitate in their responses or possibly not be able to respond at all e.g., pointing to the correct answer, writing a response, etc. Again, an inexperienced evaluator may misinterpret these reactions. There are many children falsely diagnosed with low cognitive levels, learning disabilities, etc., due to inappropriate testing techniques. Suggestions would be to talk with the school about your concerns. Be assertive about why you believe the testing may be incorrect and INSIST that an experienced evaluator retest your child. Building rapport, presenting in an informal manner, and nonverbal testing are all ways to help ease anxiety for SM children in a testing situation. In fact, presenting testing as worksheets or testing (after rapport is built) in the child's home is often an excellent way to get more accurate testing results.

(11) Since my child is so anxious in school, and is so relaxed and 'normal' at home, perhaps I should home school my child. Is this a good idea?

Unless schooling is done where there is consistent social interaction among same aged peers, I am against home schooling for SM children. A parent's good intention of helping their child by providing a comfortable, isolated setting is often postponing the inevitable; having to eventually socialize with others. If a child is home schooled in an isolated fashion and not around peers (which is necessary to build relationships and develop social skills), what is going to happen as the child ages and

has to interact in the real world and social demands become more intense? However, if home schooling is done where there are other groups of children who meet at different homes throughout the week and the child is consistently exposed to the day to day interactions of the give and take of socializing, then home schooling may be an option; especially if your only other choice is a large classroom setting where there is little individualized attention.

(12) I have a child in my class who is mute. She speaks outside the school and has two friends whom she whispers to during recess. However, for much of the day, this child sits alone and is unable to initiate interaction with others. From what I read, she seems to manifest typical SM symptoms. However, I have told the parents about Selective Mutism. They do not want to hear about it and tell me that I am over reacting. They believe (and were told by their Doctor) that their child is 'just shy,' will outgrow her shyness and is just being difficult and uncooperative. Any advice?

YES, I have plenty! Go to the website, www.selectivemutismcenter.org and print out information. We have an array of informational handouts. Please share this with the family. Encourage them to read the information and to contact our organization. Children who demonstrate true SM do not 'outgrow' their silence. What may happen to mildly SM children is that they may begin to speak quietly, but if they have not developed anxiety coping skills, their anxiety will eventually manifest itself in other ways e.g., Social Anxiety, phobias, hoarding, generalized anxiety, etc. Unfortunately too few understand the realities about SM. If a child is MUTE in school for more than a month and their mutism interferes with their ability to function academically, socially, emotionally, etc., then they have a disorder that deserves treatment. Being seen as 'difficult and uncooperative' is from someone that is not knowledgeable about SM and unfortunately may be perpetuating the unnecessary suffering this child is obviously enduring.

(13) I needed to pick my child up from school one hour early for a doctor's appointment. When I got to the school, the teacher had no idea I was coming! My daughter still had the note in her school bag. When I asked her why she had not given the note to her teacher, she just shrugged and avoided the issue. This is the second time something like this has occurred. Is this related to SM?

Yes, this is definitely an SM trait; inability to initiate when anxious. You are experiencing the fact that mutism is just one of the characteristics of our children. Also common is an inability to initiate at times. This can be something as simple as you mentioned; just handing a note to the teacher. Due to anxiety, your child is communicatively impaired. Initiation is a form of communication. Suggestions would be to speak to your treating professional to assess her ability to communicate comfortably and to work on ways to increase comfort so that initiation is less anxiety provoking

(14) My son wants so desperately to ride the bus, but can't seem to do it. I work and driving my child to school is very difficult. What can I do to help my child feel more comfortable with the bus?

Talk with your child about various options to try to help him feel more comfortable. Some suggestions are to:

- Meet the bus driver! How often do our children go to school when never officially meeting their bus drivers? Knowing that our children can be socially anxious, meeting the bus driver and spending a bit of time getting to know him/her is often enough for some kids! You can meet the bus driver at the terminal, at the school location, or at your stop (if few are on the bus), etc.
- 'Go with a friend' at first. This might mean actually going to a friend's house first so that your child has his friend to sit with.
- Visit the bus terminal to check out the bus. Bring a friend along!
- Tell your child that you will follow the bus to the school, so that when he gets off, you will be right there! This is not enabling, but merely helping your child feel more comfortable. Doing this once or twice will most likely be enough for your child to realize that the bus ride is not as scary as he thought it would be!

** It is also a good idea to talk with the bus driver and educate him/her to SM. Last thing your child needs is a bus driver that starts asking questions and totally misunderstands your child! Also, what if your child has an urgent need on the bus? These issues must be discussed.

(15) My son was making tremendous progress, and then all of a sudden he seemed to take a step back. I have no idea what happened, but two weeks ago he was talking quietly to his peers, and now nothing. Complete mutism again. What could have happened?

Obviously knowing for sure is difficult, but for children who are making progress, then slide back, reasons usually focus on heightened anxiety. Perhaps there was as situation or situations that occurred where others had too high an expectation from your child. Did others say something to him about his 'not talking' or make comments at all? Did he have a substitute teacher that may have not known about his SM? Bottom line, there is a reason why anxiety has heightened. Please speak to the teacher and find out what events occurred recently.

(16) There is a child with Selective Mutism in our 5th grade class. She participates fully, laughs, smiles and seems completely comfortable.

She does not look anxious, yet she is still not speaking in class. Can this still be the result of anxiety?

People always assume that to be anxious, you must LOOK anxious. For our children, this is not always the case. An individual with Obsessive Compulsive Disorder may wash their hands or clean the house repeatedly. He/she may not 'look' anxious, yet they have OCD and are demonstrating anxiety symptoms. Same with an individual with trichotillomania. This person may pick their skin and/or pull out hair, but they do not LOOK anxious. Compare this to an SM child who is mute. These individuals develop mutism as a means of avoiding anxious feelings. When a child is young, speaking elicits fear and therefore avoidance prevails. Eventually, you have a child who functions as your 5th grader. She can laugh, smile and communicate with ease nonverbally. However she is mute. This child is suffering from an anxiety disorder. However, their mutism may be learned, ingrained and a hard habit to break. This individual clearly should be receiving professional help to 'unlearn' her mute behavior and learn coping skills to be able to communicate more productively.

(17) My 6 yr old child refuses to go to the bathroom in school. She holds it in all day and refuses to go. She also does not go to the bathroom at friends' or relatives' houses. Although she refuses to use the bathroom in school, she has had two accidents during free play right before dismissal. What is this all about?

Sounds like your child may have a concomitant condition called paruresis or "Shy Bladder Syndrome." This is actually quite common in SM, socially anxious children. It seems like refusal when in reality your child has great anxiety about 'going' outside of the home. She is avoiding those anxious feelings by seemingly 'refusing to go.' Not going to the bathroom all day is physiologically difficult for any child. Children this age usually do not have the bladder capacity to go all day without urinating. You mentioned that both times it was during free play that the accidents occurred. Chances are she was playing, feeling relaxed and as a result, her bladder released. I recommend that you read more about Paruresis at: http://www.paruresis.org/

NOTE: Since SM kids have difficulty 'initiating' or going up to the teacher to indicate their need to use the bathroom, 'not going' or accidents may result. Either way, this is not an ideal situation for our children who have limited bladder capacity and also do not need the added pressure of wetting or soiling in front of peers! Ways to help the child begin feeling comfortable using the school bathroom are:

- Have signs or pre-written notes for presentation to the teacher to enable for direct access to the bathroom so your child can 'just go.'
- Parents should spend time in the school setting when few people are there and spend time in the bathroom. When your child goes to the bathroom, reward efforts.
- Working with a treating professional who can guide this process should be able to institute a positive reinforcement (goal=reward) system to build comfort in using the bathroom.

(18) My daughter gets hysterical when her classroom teacher is absent and there is a substitute teacher she does not know. As I work I cannot spend the whole morning at school with her. What should I do?

For our SM children, who become very attached to their teachers, having a substitute can be terrifying! When asked about substitutes, the number one concern of children who have SM is that the substitute will try to 'make them speak.' Obviously this can be quite anxiety provoking - especially if they actually had a substitute who did not understand SM and fired questions at the child. Talking with the teacher and principal about your concerns is important. They should have information about SM to give to any substitute teacher so that he/she will understand how to approach your child. In fact, you can present some of the handouts from the SMart Center website. (www.selectivemutismcenter.org) The handout, *'Helping our Teachers Understand'* is an excellent resource for all school personnel. It is a quick overview of SM that can easily be read by a substitute teacher before working with your child. Help your child to understand that there WILL be times when the teacher is absent, that all kids have substitutes at one time or another, and that their own teacher will be back in a short while. Discuss with your child what scares her about having a substitute, then talk about specific worries and help allay those fears. This will help put her mind at rest as she realizes that most of the things that scare her are 'not really that scary' at all.

(19) How can I tell if my child is genuinely sick when complaining of tummy aches, etc., or if symptoms are anxiety induced (even though there is no apparent reason for the anxiety)?

You are clearly seeing that 'mutism' is not the only symptom that characterizes our children. Physical symptoms, such as tummy aches, headaches, joint pains, and nausea are another way some of our children manifest anxiety. These symptoms often present at stressful or potentially stressful times, e.g., before going to school, parties, being separated from a parent, the day of show & tell or presentations, or during other social situations. Actually, to your child, these symptoms feel as though he/she is "really" sick. The difference is that with anxiety-related symptoms, the 'I don't feel goods' usually present at times of stress or insecurity. Also, anxious symptoms usually come and go abruptly. In other words, our children may complain of a tummy ache but think nothing of eating pizza and ice cream, or may say their leg hurts, but run down the steps to greet their Dad at the door! Real illnesses are usually accompanied by other symptoms, e.g., fever, sore throat, tiredness, low energy, lethargy. If ever you have doubts, suggestions would be to check with your child's doctor. In addition, support your child with their feelings of being sick. Let then know that you understand and explain to them WHY they may be feeling 'not so well.' Children usually do not make the connection between feeling sick and certain events. They truly feel ill. Helping them understand and offering support is just another way of helping to relieve anxious symptoms.

(20) My daughter is in Grade 1. She never spoke in pre-school and still does not speak in school. My husband still believes that she will "grow out of it" and consequently I do not have his support when I have to meet with the school to make accommodations for my daughter. How can I get the school to take ME seriously, if my own husband does not understand?

You are witnessing the reality of the situation. SM is not yet a household term. Teachers, treating professionals, family and friends may not understand at all. You are seeing this first hand. You therefore need to become as educated as possible by learning as much as you can about Selective Mutism. Make time for you and your husband to spend time together to talk. Let him know how important this meeting between the two of you is. Be confident in your approach, having preprinted information to validate your concerns and present material calmly is KEY. Approach your husband in a non-confrontational manner. The calmer you are, the more your words will impact. Let your husband know that children with SM do not just 'outgrow their silence.' You can present evidence of this by showing him letters from older teens and adults whose parents thought the same thing. Many of these people were not helped and suffer the consequences of untreated anxiety. Let him know that your child is suffering when in various social settings. I suggest that after your meeting and you have alerted him to the 'signs' of a child suffering in silence, you then take him to school, a birthday party or other social event where he can SEE your child anxious, mute and having difficulty initiating play and interacting with others. This will be painful for him and you to see, but unless your husband can SEE what you are talking about, it will be difficult for him to begin to understand. Point this behavior out to him first hand. Take him to as many social outings as possible. Having spoken to many parents, this approach (EDUCATION first, then SHOWING the child in anxious settings) has helped many dads see the situation from a different perspective. In regard to your meeting with the school, please let your husband know how important this is for your child; that you need his support here. Go to the meeting prepared; be confident, take preprinted information and state the approach that should be taken in the school. Most schools are very willing to learn (if they don't know already) and will appreciate the information you are presenting them with. Since SM is anything but rare, chances are they will be applying this information to another SM student sooner or later.

(21) When I spend time in my daughter's classroom, the other children have been questioning why 'Sally' does not speak and/or what does her voice sound like? My daughter is making progress but I can tell she is very uncomfortable about others asking these questions. Any suggestions on how I should handle these innocent yet curious questions? This situation is all too common. Actually, honesty is truly the best policy. First, talk to your daughter about these questions. By talking about the questions and discussing responses, you are preparing her for these situations that will inevitably exist. Preparation = feelings of control = less anxiety. When a child asks if 'Sally' speaks, advice is to confidently state, "Yes, Sally speaks quite a bit when she is home and other places. Speaking in school is hard for Sally." When the curious questioners ask, "WHY is talking hard?" mention that "everyone has something that makes them feel scared; perhaps it is the dark, monsters, high buildings, etc. Sally is scared to talk at times, but she is working on it, and feeling less scared lately. Just being her friend is a great way to help her feel less scared." Interestingly enough, children are usually quite satisfied with 'simple' responses. When others ask about the sound of 'Sally's' voice, just say, "Sally talks like all the other kids - like a typical girl with a really nice voice." An idea however for some SM children who are not 'too anxious' (determined with clinician's guidance) would be to tape their voice on a tape recorder for a few classmates to hear. Believe it or not, there are many SM children who will be fine with this idea! Your child may or may not want to be present when the tape is heard. You need to honor her decision on the taping. If she is completely against taping, do not push! Pushing the issue will only cause more anxiety.

(22) I have a 5 year old. She is selectively mute at school but we are making some breakthroughs. Another concern is that she is quite difficult at home. I understand that anxiety can bring on behavior problems - I've always felt that she doesn't know how to identify her emotions. Is this together with Selective Mutism, or is it another problem separate from anxiety of speaking in certain situations?

Glad to hear your child is making breakthroughs at school. This is positive! Regarding negative behaviors: YES, this is quite common, and more the norm for many of our anxious children. Unlike adults who **should** have the maturity and experience to deal with a situation, our young SM children often do not. They therefore act out behaviorally out of frustration. Something as easy as SPEAKING to most people is virtually impossible for them. This is debilitating and frustrating. Although your child is making strides, I assume she is still working through her anxiety. Perhaps the times your child is acting out the most, there is an association to a stressful social situation or feeling **out of control** feeling a **loss of control.** Characteristic of our children is their inner need for <u>control</u>. This is common with all anxieties...not just SM. Therefore GIVING your child control should help her feel less anxious and more secure. Much of this control is in the form of helping her to acknowledge and assess her feelings. This means helping her to express and gain control of her feelings. Your treatment professional should have some tactics to help your child begin and master this process. NOTE: Children with sensory processing challenges may have emotional regulation challenges, such as sensory processing challenges which lead to behavioral difficulties. Parenting skills to allow for consistency, predictability and routine are needed to help our behaviorally challenged youngsters.

(23) My 7 yr old daughter has SM. However, my husband does not want to talk to her about her mutism. He agrees she needs help, but does not want the Doctor or anyone else to talk to her about her mutism. He finally agreed on using medication, but again, does not want to tell our daughter about WHY she is taking medication. I do not agree with this approach. I believe she needs to know what is going on. Any advice?

YES - you are correct. How can a person begin to overcome something if he/she does not know what they are overcoming? Your child MUST know why she is going for help. She needs to understand her feelings of anxiety. Tactics and techniques are needed to help your child progress. Your daughter needs to be an active participant in her treatment plan. She needs to feel in control of her feelings. Knowledge = Control.

Regarding medication, this is an individual approach. Some parents are set against telling their child he/she is taking medication to help relieve anxiety, while other parents are very open and hold nothing back. Obviously, the older the child, the more curious he/she will be! For some parents, explaining to the child that he/she needs to take a vitamin is a simple and acceptable approach for many. Other children will demand more explanations. Parents are often reluctant to tell their children about medication for three main reasons:

a. They do not want their child to THINK he/she is sick or ill. Medication is something you take when you are ill. For parents that are comfortable with using the 'medication' term, it is explained to the child that the medication will help them feel less anxious. It should be noted that parents should never ever tell a child the medication will 'help him/ her speak.' Telling this to a child will just cause resistance. To the child, talking = fear!

b. Parents worry that the child will become dependent on the medication. Fortunately, this does not happen. The common medications, such as the SSRI's, are not habit forming…and since the children are not being told the medication will 'make them speak' they do not see the medication as magic bullet.

c. The parents are seeing the medication from a stigma point of view. SSRI's, the most common medications used to help our children, are ANTI-DEPRESSANTS also. This is not something that many parents handle very well. They often feel guilty, insecure and often embarrassed that THEIR pride and joy is taking a 'mental drug.' Unfortunately, this thought process only hurts the child. If a parent learnt as much as possible about these medications, they would see that their insecurity is based on their lack of understanding and knowledge of the medications. If a child had diabetes, most would not hesitate to give them insulin. If a child had strept throat, most would give antibiotics. In other words, these medications WORK, and when monitored correctly, they have minimal side effects. And since goals for medication are 9-12 months, the use is very short term

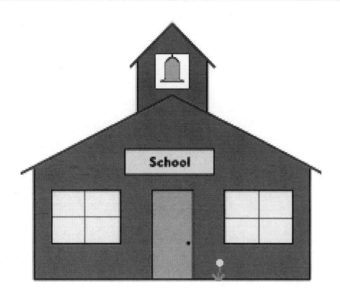

Note from the Dr. Elisa Shipon-Blum:

"Children with Selective Mutism have an excellent prognosis to overcome their social communication anxiety if diagnosed and treated early, in order to prevent learned and ingrained behavior. Treatment should focus on helping the child develop coping skills in the home, and out of the home at school and in other social settings. Understanding that Selective Mutism is a true communication anxiety where, depending on the degree of anxiety, the child may or may not be able to communicate verbally and/or nonverbally. Children with SM will not just outgrow their silence. They are not being oppositional and refusing to speak. They are crippled and stifled by their pathological reaction to social expectations. I encourage every parent, teacher and treating professional to learn as much as they can about Selective Mutism and then tell others. Chances are there are many more children suffering that any of us ever thought. The more you know, the better the chance that another child will be helped." Dr. E

Made in the USA
San Bernardino, CA
04 June 2014